James Wilson

AN INTRODUCTION TO HIS LIFE AND WORK

Introduced and Selected by Maynard Garrison

Colonial Williamsburg

The Colonial Williamsburg Foundation

Williamsburg, Virginia

20 19 18 17 16 15 14 13 12   1 2 3 4 5

Publisher's Note: The Wilson texts in part 2 of this book are taken from volume 1 of *The Collected Works of James Wilson,* published by the Liberty Fund, Indianapolis, in 2007. The Liberty Fund's primary source was the three-volume 1804 *Works of the Honourable James Wilson* prepared by Wilson's son Bird. The State House Yard Speech is reprinted with permission of the Wisconsin Historical Society.

Cover and frontispiece: *James Wilson,* by Jean Pierre Henri Elouis. Smithsonian American Art Museum, museum purchase through the Catherine Walden Myer Fund.
Page 30: Photograph by Tom Green, the Colonial Williamsburg Foundation.

Designed by Leslie Bryant Kovalic

Printed in the United States of America

Library of Congress Cataloging-in-Publication Data

Wilson, James, 1742-1798.
James Wilson : an introduction to his life and work / introduced and selected by Maynard Garrison.
p. cm.
Includes bibliographical references.
ISBN 978-0-87935-247-9 (pbk. : alk. paper)
1. Wilson, James, 1742-1798. 2. Political science—Early works to 1800.
3. Political science—United States—History—18th century. I. Garrison, Maynard, 1925– II. Colonial Williamsburg Foundation. III. Title.

JA84.U5W524 2012
973.3092—dc23
[B]
            2012011309

The Colonial Williamsburg Foundation
PO Box 1776
Williamsburg, VA 23187-1776
www.history.org

The publication of this book was made possible
by a generous gift from Henry C. Wolf.

Contents

Preface

Although a number of excellent books about James Wilson and his work have been published, his influence remains overlooked by most historians of the American Revolution and the Early Republic. This is a serious omission not only for students of American political thought but for anyone around the world who seeks the form of government championed by James Wilson during America's founding era, one based on liberty and law.

The time has come to restore James Wilson to his proper place among the true intellectual founders of America's democratic republic. This general introduction to James Wilson and several of his most important works will help build a better understanding of his many significant contributions to the creation and strengthening of the United States and of any government based on the will of the people, wherever they may be.

Part I: Life and Influence

Reburial and Recognition

Few people, certainly few Americans, more than a century after their deaths have received the tribute of respect and veneration that was paid James Wilson in 1906. In October of that year, President Theodore Roosevelt, at the dedication of Pennsylvania's new Capitol in Harrisburg, declared, "I can not do better than base my theory of governmental action upon the words and deeds of one of Pennsylvania's greatest sons, Justice James Wilson." The next month in Philadelphia, on November 22, at one thirty in the afternoon, Wilson's disinterred body, guarded by the city's famous City Troop of cavalry, was escorted several blocks to Christ Church from Independence Hall, where Wilson had lain in state for three days. The coffin, carried according to an old-time custom, was followed on foot by some of the most distinguished jurists of the day, including Melville W. Fuller, chief justice of the U.S. Supreme Court; Edward Douglass White, Oliver Wendell Holmes, and William R. Day, associate Supreme Court justices; William H. Moody, attorney general of the United States (who would also later serve on the Supreme Court); and other high federal and state officials, including members of Congress. Wilson's casket was then buried in the churchyard of Christ Church. His Pennsylvania political companion Benjamin Franklin is buried just a few blocks away in Christ Church Burial Ground.

Rarely had a more scholarly and distinguished audience of judges and government officials gathered in America to celebrate the life of someone whom they had known only through ideas, and on few occasions had a greater galaxy of speakers assembled. All had come to pay their homage and voice their tributes to the long-neglected patriot whose sheer force of intellect, more than that of almost any other single man, had, over a century before, shaped the destiny of a nation. After august religious services were conducted by Bishop Alexander Mackay-Smith, tributes were delivered from the chancel of Christ Church—where Wilson, Franklin, Thomas Jefferson, George Washington, Peyton Randolph, and others had once worshipped together—by

Pennsylvania governor Samuel W. Pennypacker; former president of the Pennsylvania Bar Association Samuel Dickson; William Draper Lewis, dean of the University of Pennsylvania Law School; the venerable Scotsman and scholar Dr. Silas Weir Mitchell; another Scotsman, the industrialist Andrew Carnegie; Alton B. Parker, the president of the American Bar Association; U.S. senator Philander C. Knox, who spoke for Congress; Supreme Court Justice White, who represented the federal judiciary; and Attorney General Moody. Hampton L. Carson, attorney general of Pennsylvania and historian of the U.S. Supreme Court, delivered the oration. All paid their respects to the man who had done so much to create the constitution they all served.

In an article describing the ceremony, Lucien Hugh Alexander, a Philadelphia lawyer who played a leading role in returning Wilson's body to Philadelphia, stated:

> Our nation is yet in its infancy, and it is probable that a hundred, three hundred, or five hundred years hence, when the perspective of time shall have adjusted the proportions, two great figures will loom from the Revolutionary period, the one, Wilson's, whose brain conceived and created the nation; the other, Washington's, who wielded the physical forces that made it. While doubtless the affections of Americans will always be centered in Washington as "the father of his country," the world at large will be apt to place one above the other, and as to which will receive the laurel wreath of highest fame will probably depend upon whether at that distant day a man who wielded the physical forces will be deemed equal to the man who swayed the intellectual forces of his time. But however this may be, James Wilson's fame is secure as the greatest intellectual power dominating the nation at its birth, and his services to our people, his doctrines and governmental theories are destined, in the oncoming years, more and more to receive popular recognition; for we live in an age of research, and they cannot escape the attention they deserve.

Alexander was not overstating the case for Wilson. Even a cursory review of the ideas and events that created the United States from 1768 through 1795 reveals the magnitude and significance of Wilson's contributions. He and his ideas played a seminal role throughout the period, as reflected in the fact that he was one of only six persons to sign both the Declaration of Independence and the Constitution. Except for the reburial ceremony in November 1906, Wilson has never been properly recognized as the one "whose brain conceived and created the nation" and who "swayed the intellectual forces of his time." He is given only passing reference in the standard historical texts. Even when he died, in 1798, the newspapers of Philadelphia failed to so much as mention his passing. Perhaps his persistent financial troubles and two brief jail terms for unpaid debts were unacceptable to pietistic early historians. And then there was the delay of fifty years in publishing James Madison's notes of the Constitutional Convention—this silence allowed others to claim or assign credit for Wilson's dominance of the convention without any refutation.

Yet James Wilson . . .

In 1774 published his most important political pamphlet, "Considerations on the Nature and Extent of the Legislative Authority of the British Parliament," which was, with works by Thomas Jefferson and John Adams, among the earliest and most forceful arguments against Parliament's sovereignty over the internal affairs of the American colonies.

From 1775 to 1787 frequently worked in the Continental Congress to promote the economic growth and political health of the infant nation.

In 1787 was one of the most influential delegates to the Constitutional Convention. He spoke 168 times, second only to Gouverneur Morris. His ideas were as authoritative as James Madison's (and much more so than Alexander Hamilton's).

In 1787 delivered his State House Yard Speech, which answered Anti-Federalist critics of the Constitution throughout the nation just as effectively as the more well-known Federalist Papers.

In 1789 was appointed by George Washington as an associate justice to the first U.S. Supreme Court. His most significant opinion, in 1793, helped establish popular sovereignty as a fundamental American principle and preceded John Marshall's opinion in *Marbury v. Madison* by ten years.

In 1790, as one of America's first professors of law, began to deliver a series of lectures at the College of Philadelphia, now the University of Pennsylvania, on the Constitution and American law in general, which laid a powerful and influential philosophical foundation for the development of any government based on the will of the people.

From Scotland to America

James Wilson was born near St. Andrews, Scotland, on September 14, 1742, the son of a farmer and one of several children in humble circumstances. The household of a farmer might, in those days, have been a healthy life, but it was bound to have been a hard one. Methods of husbandry were crude, there was little variety of produce, even fertile soil was not constituted to yield lavish crops, and after the rent had been met there was little left. Dwellings were small and bare, furnishings were meager and rude. Nevertheless, a boy with intelligence and grit could find opportunities.

At the age of fifteen, he earned a scholarship to the United College of St. Salvator and St. Leonard, part of the University of St. Andrews. Although he began as an arts student, he then decided to prepare for a life in the Presbyterian church. But his later writings reveal that he entertained much broader interests, including classical government and philosophy. Wilson was profoundly influenced by the leading lights of the Scottish Enlightenment, thinkers such as Adam Smith and Thomas Reid at Glasgow and Hugh Blair at Edinburgh. They contributed to his grounding in logic and rhetoric, two arts that he practiced with conspicuous mastery in his future career.

For approximately two decades in the eighteenth century, Scotland produced more than a dozen of the most important men in the history of Western philosophy. Benjamin Franklin, after a visit to Scotland and reading some of their works, called them "a Set of as truly great Men . . . as have ever appeared in any Age or Country." In addition to Smith and Reid, they included Francis Hutcheson, Lord Kames, and David Hume.

America was fortunate to become familiar with their works primarily through another Scot, John Witherspoon, a Presbyterian minister from Paisley who was persuaded to immigrate to America to become the president of the College of New Jersey, now Princeton University. For twenty-five years, Witherspoon required his students to study the works of men who formed the core of what was known as the Scottish Enlightenment. Among his students were the future president James Madison, six governors, eight college presidents, and over one hundred ministers. Their influence is impossible to evaluate.

Before leaving Scotland in 1765, Wilson encountered the work of both Francis Hutcheson and Thomas Reid. He extolled Reid's common sense and thought him a natural partner of popular sovereignty. Wilson observed that the entire basis of the rule of law in a democratic society under the doctrine of popular sovereignty was "the consent of those whose obedience the law requires." He endorsed Reid's view that the common man was "a man of integrity" who "sees his duty without reasoning, as he sees the highway." Wilson came to trust people to do the right thing, particularly the American people.

The jury system was his model, not just for how the law works in a free society but for how democracy works as well. Its fundamental building block was man as knower and as judger, a person who trusts his own senses and who grasps facts and grasps right and wrong, a person who can recognize when he has the solution to a problem, or someone else does, and who goes along with what the majority finally decides.

Wilson believed that as long as the individual heeded these perceptions of "common" sense, available to all, he could function as a valuable and responsible citizen of a republic. This view caused him to fight on every possible occasion, from the Continental Congress to the Constitutional Convention to the U.S. Supreme Court, for the broadest popular base for the government of the United States. He urged that not only representatives but also the senators and the president should be separately elected by the people.

In the beginning of 1765, Wilson embarked on his journey across the Atlantic, where opportunities for an ambitious young Scot abounded. He arrived at New York in June. This was a critical juncture in American history as the debate over the Stamp Act began to rage. Wilson immediately traveled to Philadelphia. He got a job teaching Latin at the College of Philadelphia, now the University of Pennsylvania, having impressed the trustees by his classical scholarship and the all-around quality of his education. The school had seventy or eighty pupils, and Wilson's qualities as a teacher seem to have been recognized and respected by the boys who came under his guidance. Still, even though the college awarded him an honorary master's degree in 1766, he remained there only a few months before finding an opening as a student of the law in the office of John Dickinson, a leading lawyer of

Philadelphia and one of America's most influential political thinkers. After applying himself wholeheartedly to the study of law, Wilson was admitted to the Pennsylvania bar in 1767. He began practicing law, first in Reading and later, by 1770, in Carlisle.

At that time, the British North American colonies occupied the fringe on the eastern seaboard of the continent. Their free and enslaved population did not greatly exceed two million, and, on the whole, the practical administration of the colonies was left to the colonists and their representative assemblies. Loyalty to the British Crown and to the British constitution was strong, but many people began to see that the policies enacted by the British Parliament were unconstitutional and therefore a danger to their interests and freedoms. Independence, however, faced many obstacles. For one, the colonies were jealous of one another; their rivalries frustrated free trade, and they differed greatly in religious notions and habits. They could hardly be persuaded to cooperate for mutual defense against either the inroads of Native American tribes or the aggressions of the French, two of the most serious problems of the colonial period, let alone unite for American independence from Britain.

Many were united, however, by their reaction to news from London about the Stamp Act. Intended to pay for the cost of protecting the American colonies, the act had been passed by the Houses of Parliament, had received the royal assent, and would go into force on November 1, 1765. The leading British minister, George Grenville, with the support of King George III and a majority in the British Parliament, had decided to take control of imperial affairs. They had had enough of colonial governments that refused to contribute to the enormous debt incurred by the Seven Years' War.

The Stamp Act was not the first indication of parliamentary intentions to take more aggressive action in colonial affairs. The British government had already provoked irritation and vigorous resistance in New England by two earlier measures of administration: an instruction to customs officers to act rigorously against smuggling on the American seaboard and the issuance of writs of assistance, giving customs officers exceedingly wide powers to search for contraband goods. New Englanders wrote remonstrances to both Parliament and the king, but they had been largely disregarded, and the measures themselves were actively enforced with seemingly arrogant indifference to what many colonists deemed to be their rights as English subjects.

The Stamp Act went further. It not only impacted every colony, but it was intended to levy a tax on the internal commerce and business of the colonies, violating the constitutional authority hitherto exercised by the elected colonial assemblies. Resentment against the measure, as an infringement of constitutional liberty, was immediate and almost universal.

The statute imposed a stamp duty on most written instruments required to conduct business and was meant to raise revenue that would contribute to paying off a massive British national debt amassed partly to protect the colonies. James Otis, the Boston orator, made an impassioned declaration against the right of Parliament to pass acts for revenue. This was a way, he argued, of extracting money from a citizen without his consent: in other words, it was "taxation without representation." In Otis's impassioned words lay the roots of colonial rebellion against the mother country—and the development of one of the most important principles of American constitutional theory.

It was during the tumultuous years that followed that James Wilson entered politics, publishing essays and pamphlets that presented new ideas about relationships between governments and the governed, including several of his 1768 articles and his 1774 piece "Considerations on the Nature and Extent of the Legislative Authority of the British Parliament," which forcefully pushed the colonial argument that Parliament had no authority over the colonies. It numbered Wilson firmly among the patriots and contributed to his election to the Continental Congress, which on July 2, 1776, made the decision for independence. The Declaration of Independence, drafted primarily by Thomas Jefferson, substantially edited by Congress, was clearly influenced by Wilson's "Considerations." The Declaration was signed on the part of Pennsylvania by Franklin, Wilson, Benjamin Rush, George Clymer, and Robert Morris. Wilson faced the deeply troubling separation from Britain with ample foresight and did all he could, through his writings and his arguments, to make it a reality.

From the Continental Congress to the Constitutional Convention

After the Declaration of Independence was signed, Congress found it essential to devise a plan for combined action by the thirteen new individual states. Several devices were suggested. John Dickinson proposed the Articles of Confederation, adopted by Congress in November 1777. In the ensuing discussion, Wilson pointed out that representation of each state should be regulated according to the number of free men. If any government should speak the will of all the people, it would be perfect, he maintained; and, so far as it might depart from that, it would become relatively imperfect. He argued that the objects in the care of Congress were not the states but their individual inhabitants. Merely to annex the term *state* to ten thousand men should not give them equal political weight with forty thousand. Where matters referred to Congress were concerned, the many states were but one large state. The states lay aside their individual interests, Wilson maintained, as when they assemble in a federal congress, which then ought to proceed in accordance with the interests of the majority.

For such ideas the members of Congress were not ready. The votes in Congress were the votes not of the individual delegates but of the states they represented and were inoperative until they had been confirmed by the state legislatures; and to every financial measure the consent of at least nine states, declared in each case by a majority of the state delegates, was necessary. The executive power of Congress was severely limited. The states alone could carry Congress's resolutions into effect, each acting independently within its own boundaries. This system was a source of difficulties, hindrances, and weakness throughout the Revolutionary War and long after the conflict was over.

Despite the difficulties of conducting business in the Continental Congress, Wilson dedicated himself vigorously to its business. He served on many committees and was never known to refuse an assignment.

Wilson's primary fame rests on his contributions in the fields of government and law, but, in the years 1780 to 1786, he was in the forefront of an effort to put the economy of the United States on a sound basis. In the course of the establishing of the Bank of North America, Wilson revealed his views not only regarding finance but on a broad range of economic policy.

Wilson's general view of economic policy was largely derived from two distinguished Scottish economists of the eighteenth century—Adam Smith, whose book *An Inquiry into the Nature and Causes of the Wealth of Nations* Wilson thoroughly absorbed and whose influence is frequently evident in his observations on economic matters, and, more notably, Sir James Steuart, whose monumental work *An Inquiry into the Principles of Political Economy* had a profound effect on Wilson. To Wilson, there seemed to be striking similarities between the economic needs of his native Scotland in the late seventeenth and early eighteenth centuries and those of his adopted America in the later eighteenth century. As in other fields, many of Wilson's economic ideas emerged from the broader influence of the Scottish Enlightenment in its many guises. One such was Steuart's view that adequate credit facilities were the key to rapid economic development, especially in underdeveloped countries, which the United States undoubtedly was in the late 1700s.

The Bank of North America was the first bank in the modern sense in the United States. James Wilson was intimately involved with the bank's creation and its subsequent operation. The bank would provide a more effective circulating medium, as well as facilities for raising loans either by private individuals or by the government. Wilson's contribution to the emergence of a more effective banking system was, in its own right, of major importance. In a real sense, he anticipated, in his economic ideas and their constitutional corollaries, the work of Alexander Hamilton twenty years later.

Wilson's next major contribution to the foundation of the United States was his role as a leading architect of the Constitution as a delegate to the Constitutional Convention in Philadelphia in 1787. An accurate study of the creation of the Constitution by the fifty-five delegates is severely hampered by the first act of that assembly: their solemnly sworn pact of secrecy regarding all the matters to come before them. To a very substantial degree the delegates honored that pact, and not until the death of James Madison in

1840 were his exhaustive notes made public and an accurate report of what the delegates accomplished made possible. In the intervening years, heroes of the Constitution were created in the public mind, unfairly enlarging the roles of some men, such as Alexander Hamilton, who were rarely present or who made minor contributions. Others who were more deserving, such as Wilson, were ignored. Madison's notes reveal that Wilson was intimately involved in every aspect of the creation, ultimately gave 168 speeches, and was regarded by many as second only to Madison as the most profound scholar of the convention.

The months of the convention, stretching from May to the middle of September 1787, were the greatest of Wilson's life and perhaps represent his greatest ongoing contribution to American history. It was here that his mind, honed by the thoughts and words of his teachers and his adversaries, was able to deal day after day with the fundamental issues of government. Forced in the convention to speak extemporaneously or with a minimum of preparation, he was driven by circumstance from the elaborate manner of his formal orations into a spare, agile, and effective style. Partly as a result of his effectiveness, the Constitution was adopted on September 17.

After the rules of procedure had been adopted, the Constitutional Convention of 1787 came immediately to the very heart of the problem that it had met to consider. Edmund Randolph, governor of Virginia, rose to present the Virginia Resolves. Those resolves bore the mark of James Madison's incisive mind, as did much of the reasoning that supported them. As presented by Randolph, they expressed the aspirations of the large states, who felt it only fair for them to be represented in any new government in direct proportion to their populations.

Randolph proposed a two-house legislature: the lower house to be elected by the people of the states, the upper house to be elected by the lower, and they together would elect the executive. The new legislature ought to be empowered to act in all cases where the individual states were unable to act effectively. A national judiciary would be established with judges who would hold office only "during good behavior." Provision should be made for the admission of new states; a republican form of government should be guaranteed to every state and territory. Randolph concluded with an exhortation to the delegates to make good use of their opportunity to frame a strong and rational government. After he had seated himself, the convention resolved to form itself into a committee of the whole "to consider of the state of the American Union." Next day, May 30, the convention began its consideration of the Virginia Plan.

There was widespread agreement that any new national legislature should comprise two branches. This was orthodox wisdom, with which Wilson fully concurred, and was based on the grounds that a bicameral legislature was a defense against legislative tyranny. In support of Madison's argument in favor of the election of one branch by the people, Wilson struck the keynote of what was to be a frequent refrain. Madison reported:

> Mr. Wilson contended strenuously for drawing the most numerous branch of the Legislature immediately from the people. He was for raising the federal pyramid to a considerable altitude, and for that reason wished to give it as broad a basis as possible. No government could long subsist without the confidence of the people. In a republican Government this confidence was peculiarly essential. He also thought it wrong to increase the weight of the State Legislatures by making them the electors of the national Legislature. All interference between the general and local Governmts. should be obviated as much as possible. On examination it would be found that the opposition of States to federal measures had proceded much more from the officers of the States, than from the people at large.

On the question of election to the second branch, Madison reported:

> Mr. Wilson opposed both a nomination by the State Legislatures, and an election by the first branch of the national Legislature, because the second branch of the latter, ought to be independent of both. He thought both branches of the National Legislature ought to be chosen by the people, but was not prepared with a specific proposition.

Wilson's solution was to create electoral districts composed of groups of districts for election to the lower house, transcending state boundaries if necessary when a small state was concerned. Had it been implemented, it would have given powerful support to the concept of a popular basis for the national government. But, as Wilson quickly realized, it was a suggestion far too revolutionary to have any hope of adoption; not only was it incompatible with prevailing concepts of state dignity, it was also inconsistent with the still predominant view that the upper house should differ in its general nature from the lower. Seeing the impossibility of gaining what he really wanted, Wilson changed his position. Though Wilson's idea of electors was not implemented in electing members of Congress, this remarkable proposal, made in late May 1787, was ultimately adopted on September 6, 1787, as the best means of electing the president. The Electoral College is still in action today. Also, Wilson's original idea of direct election of the senators by the people was adopted in 1913 as the Seventeenth Amendment to the Constitution.

The question of the form the executive branch of government should take involved fewer fundamental issues, though the technical problems were highly complex. Controversy over the executive turned primarily on its nature and composition—whether it should consist of a single person or of more than one; the manner in which it should be appointed, which turned out to be the greatest technical difficulty the convention had to face (solved in part by the idea of electors); and what powers it should have.

Madison reported:

> Mr. Wilson preferred a single magistrate, as giving most energy dispatch and responsibility to the office. He did not consider the Prerogatives of the British Monarch as a proper guide in defining the Executive powers. . . . The only powers he conceived strictly Executive were those of executing the laws, and appointing officers, not appertaining to and appointed by the Legislature.

Wilson believed that the executive branch should be independent but that its powers should be commensurate with those of the other two branches. Although he was always acutely conscious of the danger of legislative tyranny, he was not thereby tempted to inflate the powers of the executive as a counterbalance. Whereas in the discussions over the legislative branch he was always pushing hard to achieve a high degree of power and independence for the national government in relation to the states, in the discussions over the executive branch he did not display the same determination to strengthen the executive at the expense of the legislative branch. His concern was that the executive be appointed by the people; this would give the executive authority to maintain its independence. Madison reported:

> He wished to derive not only both branches of the Legislature from the people, without the intervention of the State Legislatures but the Executive also; in order to make them as independent as possible of each other, as well as of the States.

Wilson's view was not merely that the three branches of government be independent of one another. He also held that their influence should be as nearly equal as could be. He was particularly sensitive about the position of the judicial branch, and he strove on every appropriate occasion to ensure for the judiciary the influence to which he thought it entitled. He never, for instance, doubted that one of the primary responsibilities of the judiciary was that of judicial review.

After two months of deliberation the delegates believed that many of the issues had been agreed on and that the best way to proceed was with a draft before them that they could analyze and review. They elected five members to act as the Committee of Detail, which included Wilson, Edmund Randolph, and John Rutledge. After two weeks of drafting, review, and amendment, the final report, largely shaped by Wilson, provided the principal elements of the ultimately adopted system: the delegation and enumeration of federal legislative powers, the jurisdictional demarcation of the powers of the federal courts, the "necessary and proper" clause, and the supremacy clause.

On August 6, 1787, the printed proposal of the Committee of Detail was distributed to each delegate for his consideration. For the next five weeks, the printed proposal was examined and reviewed, and, although other additions and alterations were made, the essential content of the Constitution as prepared by James Wilson and the committee was adopted as the Constitution for the United States and ultimately signed by thirty-nine delegates on September 17, 1787.

The Constitutional Convention came to an end on that date. Before it ended, the convention considered what should be done with the journals and so forth, whether members should be allowed copies. It was resolved "that he [George Washington, president of the convention] retain the Journal and other papers, subject to the order of the Congress, if ever formed under the Constitution."

Wilson then led the effort in Pennsylvania to see that the Constitution was ratified by the people, a campaign so successful that his most memorable public address—the State House Yard Speech—was credited with influencing ratification in other states.

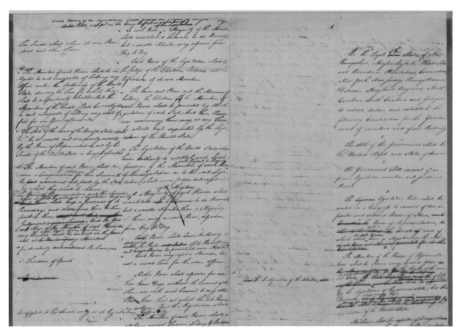

One of the earliest surviving drafts of the first page of the Constitution handwritten in 1787 by James Wilson. The Historical Society of Pennsylvania (HSP), Treasures Collection.

Lawyer and Judge

O nce the Constitution was ratified, and he successfully worked for a new Pennsylvania Constitution, Wilson settled down to more philosophical pursuits. In 1790, the College of Philadelphia, later the University of Pennsylvania, made Wilson the college's first law professor. The college charged him with giving a series of lectures; these would secure his legacy through a thorough explanation and analysis of the Constitution and the legal system on which it was based. As one of America's most prominent legal scholars of the time, he would place the Constitution in its proper context, that is, as a result of a general theory of government and politics.

The way was thus opened for Wilson to expound on his often emphasized view of the uniqueness of the American system. He believed there had been nothing like it in the history of the world, and therefore there were no precedents to serve as a guide. Above all, the nature of the principle of democracy enshrined in it went far beyond anything before attempted and was therefore uniquely American. The principle of direct representation, which was an essential element in the Constitution, had never been successfully applied anywhere in its pure form. The ancient world did not have any understanding of it, and the British constitution reflected it only indirectly. He believed that in Britain the executive and judicial branches were not based even indirectly on the principle of representation, and even in the legislative branch "it does not predominate; though it may serve as a check." In the British constitution, the principle of representation was therefore confined to "a narrow corner," though it extended further than in any other European government. Wilson chose to emphasize not the utility of the Constitution in relation to the needs of the United States but the fact that it emanated wholly from the people. He stressed:

> If we take an extended and accurate view of it, we shall find the streams of power running in different directions, in different dimensions, and at different heights, watering, adorning, and

> fertilizing the fields and meadows, through which their courses
> are led; but if we trace them, we shall discover, that they all
> originally flow from one abundant fountain. In this constitution,
> all authority is derived from the people.

He gave a number of the lectures, but the series was never completed because on September 26, 1789, the U.S. Senate confirmed Wilson's appointment by President George Washington as an associate justice to the first Supreme Court of the United States. Although his lectures were not completed, the texts were published by his son Bird in 1804. They constituted a solid constitutional interpretation to guide the new republic. While their exact contribution to the growth, acceptance, and nurturing of the new republic is impossible to measure, it can be safely said that they were essential. They were a basic part of legal training throughout the United States for many years after.

George Washington appointed Wilson to the Supreme Court because he greatly admired Wilson's intelligence and said so publicly. As most Americans know, one of the significant checks and balances incorporated in the U.S.'s form of government is the power of the judiciary to declare acts of other branches of the federal government unconstitutional. The salutary effect of this doctrine is accepted today, but it was the subject of heated debate for several years after ratification. It is a commonly accepted position today that the doctrine was established by Chief Justice John Marshall in 1803 in the case *Marbury v. Madison* in which the court established its authority to declare an act of Congress unconstitutional. Almost totally overlooked, however, is the opinion of James Wilson in *Chisholm v. Georgia* in 1793, ten years before *Marbury v. Madison*. In this case, Wilson examined the highly charged question of judicial review by the federal Supreme Court of an action by a state. The right of the judiciary to exercise jurisdiction over the state of Georgia was regarded as so unwarranted that Georgia declined to respond to a properly served summons and complaint by a citizen of South Carolina. In holding Georgia accountable to judicial review, Wilson elegantly wrote:

> Whoever considers, in a combined and comprehensive view,
> the general texture of the Constitution, will be satisfied, that
> the people of the United States intended to form themselves

into a nation for national purposes. They instituted, for such purposes, a national Government, complete in all its parts, with powers Legislative, Executive and Judiciary; and, in all those powers, extending over the whole nation. Is it congruous, that, with regard to such purposes, any man or body of men, any person natural or artificial, should be permitted to claim successfully an entire exemption from the jurisdiction of the national Government? Would not such claims, crowned with success, be repugnant to our very existence as a nation? When so many trains of deduction, coming from different quarters, converge and unite, at last, in the same point; we may safely conclude, as the legitimate result of this Constitution, that the State of Georgia is amenable to the jurisdiction of this Court.

The decision remains the highlight of his career on the court. Unfortunately, his financial difficulties curtailed a promising judicial career. For many of the years of his public duties, Wilson was also a successful practicing lawyer earning a substantial income. His income permitted him to engage in an aggressive investment program to share in the benefits of the emerging new nation. His investments included a lumber mill, an iron furnace, a nail and wire factory, and several homes. Mostly, however, he purchased warrants to buy real estate, which required regular payments of interest plus the cost of perfecting title. That burden finally caused Wilson's economic downfall. While he was earning a considerable income as a practicing lawyer, he could meet his financial demands, but, on a Supreme Court justice's salary of three thousand dollars per annum, he could not. Nevertheless, despite his deteriorating financial condition, Wilson never lost faith in the ultimate success of the American economy and, in fact, continued to invest.

In the late eighteenth century, imprisonment for debt was standard practice. In 1797, Wilson was heavily in debt and unable to meet obligations to creditors. Although a sitting Supreme Court justice, he was arrested and imprisoned for two brief periods until his son Bird was able to gather sufficient funds to secure his release. He is the only sitting justice to have been so imprisoned. A year later, after his father's death, Bird Wilson was able to pay the bulk of the debts in full.

Wilson died on August 28, 1798, at Edenton, North Carolina, at the home of James Iredell, his friend and colleague on the bench of the Supreme Court of the United States. Iredell died shortly after and was buried beside Wilson.

One of the most appreciative of Wilson's latter-day admirers was a fellow Scot, James Bryce, an able and influential European expositor and interpreter of the American political system. Bryce had no doubt of Wilson's eminence—perhaps even preeminence—as a Founding Father, and he wrote what remains the most perceptive of all tributes to him:

> The services which such a mind as Wilson's, broad, penetrating, exact, and luminous can render to a nation can hardly be overestimated. In the long run, the world is ruled by ideas. Whoever gives a nation, and most of all to a nation at the outset of its career, sound just principles for the conduct of its government, principles which are in harmony with its character and are capable of progressive expansion as it expands, is a true benefactor to that nation, and deserves to be held in everlasting memory. Such a one was James Wilson.

Part II: Writings and Speeches

Considerations on the Nature and Extent of the Legislative Authority of the British Parliament

In 1768, when tension between the colonies and Britain was at its highest, Wilson undertook to study the legal relationship between the British Parliament and the colonies and between the British king and the colonies. He entitled the study *Considerations on the Nature and Extent of the Legislative Authority of the British Parliament.* Even though Wilson began his study with the assumption that acts of Parliament had at least some binding effect in the colonies, he was amazed to discover in the works he studied and sphere of constitutional thought in which he was immersed that he could find no sufficient basis for that assumption. His thorough analysis is accompanied by notes and references, and his conclusions, he believed, were thoroughly supported by legal decisions of the highest courts even if most of his contemporaries, with their own evidence, legal philosophy, and constitutional precedents, disagreed. It remains one of the most influential political pamphlets of the Revolutionary period and clearly, in his statement of the basic natural rights doctrine of popular sovereignty, influenced the Declaration of Independence.

Confiderationſ on the *Nature* and *Extent* of the Legiſlative Authority of the Britiſh Parliament, 1774

No question can be more important to Great Britain, and to the colonies, than this—does the legislative authority of the British parliament extend over them?

On the resolution of this question, and on the measures which a resolution of it will direct, it will depend, whether the parent country, like a happy mother, shall behold her children flourishing around her, and receive the most grateful returns for her protection and love; or whether, like a step dame, rendered miserable by her own unkind conduct, she shall see their affections alienated, and herself deprived of those advantages which a milder treatment would have ensured to her.

The British nation are generous: they love to enjoy freedom: they love to behold it: slavery is their greatest abhorrence. Is it possible, then, that they would wish themselves the authors of it? No. Oppression is not a plant of the British soil; and the late severe proceedings against the colonies must have arisen from the detestable schemes of interested ministers, who have misinformed and misled the people. A regard for that nation, from whom we have sprung, and from whom we boast to have derived the spirit which prompts us to oppose their unfriendly measures, must lead us to put this construction on what we have lately seen and experienced. When, therefore, they shall know and consider the justice of our claim—that we insist only upon being treated as freemen, and as the descendants of those British ancestors, whose memory we will not dishonour by our degeneracy, it is reasonable to hope, that they will approve of our conduct, and bestow their loudest applauses on our congenial ardour for liberty.

But if these reasonable and joyful hopes should fatally be disappointed, it will afford us at least some satisfaction to know, that the principles on which we have founded our opposition to the late acts of parliament, are the principles of justice and freedom, and of the British constitution. If our righteous struggle shall be attended with misfortunes, we will reflect with exultation on the noble cause of them; and while suffering unmerited distress, think ourselves superiour to the proudest slaves. On the contrary, if we shall be reinstated in the enjoyment of those rights, to which we are entitled by the supreme and uncontrollable laws of nature, and the fundamental principles of the British constitution, we shall reap the glorious fruit of our labours; and we shall, at the same time, give to the world and to posterity an instructive example, that the cause of liberty ought not to be despaired of, and that a generous contention in that cause is not always unattended with success.

The foregoing considerations have induced me to publish a few remarks on the important question, with which I introduced this essay.

Those who allege that the parliament of Great Britain have power to make laws binding the American colonies, reason in the following manner. "That there is and must be in every state a supreme, irresistible, absolute, uncontrolled authority, in which the *jura summi imperii*, or the rights of sovereignty, reside:"[a] "That this supreme power is, by the constitution of Great Britain, vested in the king, lords, and commons:"[b] "That, therefore, the acts of the king, lords, and commons, or, in other words, acts of parliament, have, by the British constitution, a binding force on the American colonies, they composing a part of the British empire."

I admit that the principle, on which this argument is founded, is of great importance: its importance, however, is derived from its tendency to promote the ultimate end of all government. But if the application of it would, in any instance, destroy, instead of promoting, that end, it ought, in that instance, to be rejected: for to admit it, would be to sacrifice the end to the means, which are valuable only so far as they advance it.

All men are, by nature, equal and free: no one has a right to any authority over another without his consent: all lawful government is founded on the consent of those who are subject to it: such consent was given with a view to ensure and to increase the happiness of the governed, above what they could enjoy in an independent and unconnected state of nature. The consequence is, that the happiness of the society is the *first* law of every government.[c]

This rule is founded on the law of nature: it must control every political maxim: it must regulate the legislature itself.[d] The people have a right to insist that this rule be observed; and are entitled to demand a moral security that the legislature will observe it. If they have not the first, they are slaves; if they have not the second, they are, every moment, exposed to slavery. For "civil liberty is nothing else but natural liberty, devested of that part which constituted the independence of individuals, by the authority which it confers on sovereigns, attended with a right of insisting upon their making a good use of their authority, and with a moral security that this right will have its effect."[e]

Let me now be permitted to ask—Will it ensure and increase the happiness of the American colonies, that the parliament of Great Britain should possess a supreme, irresistible, uncontrolled authority over them? Is such an authority consistent with their liberty? Have they any security that it will be employed only for their good? Such a security is absolutely necessary. Parliaments are not infallible: they are not always just. The members, of whom they are composed, are human; and, therefore, they may err; they are influenced by interest; and, therefore, they may deviate from their duty. The acts of the body must depend upon the opinions and dispositions of the members: the acts of the body may, then, be the result of errour and of vice. It is no breach of decency to suppose all this: the British constitution supposes it: "it supposes that parliaments may betray their trust, and provides, as far as human wisdom can provide, that they may not be able to do so long, without a sufficient control."[f] Without provisions for this purpose, the temple of British liberty, like a structure of ice, would instantly dissolve before the fire of oppression and despotick sway.

It will be very material to consider the several securities, which the inhabitants of Great Britain have, that their liberty will not be destroyed by the legislature, in whose hands it is intrusted. If it shall appear, that the same securities are not enjoyed by the colonists; the undeniable consequence will be, that the colonists are not under the same obligations to intrust their liberties into the hands of the same legislature: for the colonists are entitled to all[g] the privileges of Britons. We have committed no crimes to forfeit them: we have too much spirit to resign them. We will leave our posterity as free as our ancestors left us.

To give to any thing that passes in parliament the force of a law, the consent of the king, of the lords, and of the commons[h] is absolutely necessary.[i] If, then, the inhabitants of Great Britain possess a sufficient restraint upon any of these branches of the legislature, their liberty is secure, provided they be not wanting to themselves. Let us take a view of the restraints, which they have upon the house of commons.

They elect the members of that house. "Magistrates," says Montesquieu,[j] "are properly theirs, who have the nomination of them." The members of the house of commons, therefore, elected by the people, are the magistrates of the people; and are bound by the ties of gratitude for the honour and confidence conferred upon them, to consult the interest of their constituents.

The power of elections has ever been regarded as a point of the last consequence to all[k] free governments. The independent exercise of that power is justly deemed the strongest bulwark of the British liberties.[l] As such, it has always been an object of great attention to the legislature; and is expressly stipulated with the prince in the bill of rights. All those are excluded from voting, whose poverty is such, that they cannot live independent, and must therefore be subject to the undue influence of their superiours. Such are supposed to have no will of their own: and it is judged improper that they should vote in the representation of a free state. What can exhibit in a more striking point of view, the peculiar care which has been taken, in order to render the election of members of parliament entirely free? It was deemed an insult upon the independent commons of England, that their uninfluenced suffrages should be adulterated by those who were not at liberty to speak as they thought, though their interests and inclinations were the same. British liberty, it was thought, could not be effectually secured, unless those who made the laws were freely, and without influence, elected by those for whom they were made. Upon this principle is reasonably founded the maxim in law—that every one, who is capable of exercising his will, is party, and presumed to consent, to an act of parliament.

For the same reason that persons, who live dependent upon the will of others, are not admitted to vote in elections, those who are under age, and therefore incapable of judging; those who are convicted of perjury or subornation of perjury, and therefore unworthy of judging; and those who obtain their freeholds by fraudulent conveyances, and would therefore vote to serve infamous purposes, are all likewise excluded from the enjoyment of this great privilege. Corruption at elections is guarded against by the strictest precautions, and most severe penalties. Every elector, before he polls, must, if demanded by a candidate or by two electors, take the oath against bribery, as prescribed by 2. Geo. 2. c. 24. Officers of the excise, of the customs, and of the post offices; officers concerned in the duties upon leather, soap, paper, striped linens imported, hackney coaches, cards and dice, are restrained from interfering in elections, under the penalty of one hundred pounds, and of being incapable of ever exercising any office of trust under the king.

Thus is the freedom of elections secured from the servility, the ignorance, and the corruption of the electors; and from the interposition of officers depending immediately upon the crown. But this is not all. Provisions, equally salutary, have been made concerning the qualifications of those who shall be elected. All imaginable care has been taken, that the commons of Great Britain may be neither awed, nor allured, nor deceived into any nomination inconsistent with their liberties.

It has been adopted as a general maxim, that the crown will take advantage of every opportunity of extending its prerogative, in opposition to the privileges of the people; that it is the interest of those who have pensions or offices at will from the crown, to concur in all its measures; that mankind in general will prefer their private interest to the good of their country; and that, consequently, those who enjoy such pensions or offices are unfit to represent a free nation, and to have the care of their liberties committed to their hands.[m] All such officers or pensioners are declared incapable of being elected members of the house of commons.

But these are not the only checks which the commons of Great Britain have, upon the conduct of those whom they elect to represent them in parliament. The interest of the representatives is the same with that of their constituents. Every measure, that is prejudicial to the nation, must be prejudicial to them and their posterity. They cannot betray their electors, without, at the same time, injuring themselves. They must join in bearing the burthen of every oppressive act; and participate in the happy effects of every wise and good law. Influenced by these considerations, they will seriously and with attention examine every measure proposed to them; they will behold it in every light, and extend their views to its most distant consequences. If, after the most mature deliberation, they find it will be conducive to the welfare of their country, they will support it with ardour: if, on the contrary, it appears to be of a dangerous and destructive nature, they will oppose it with firmness.

Every social and generous affection concurs with their interest, in animating the representatives of the commons of Great Britain to an honest and faithful discharge of their important trust. In each patriotick effort, the heart-felt satisfaction of having acted a worthy part vibrates in delightful unison with the applause of their countrymen, who never fail to express their warmest acknowledgements to the friends and bene- factors of their country. How pleasing are those rewards! How much to be preferred to that paltry wealth, which is sometimes procured by meanness and treachery! I say sometimes; for meanness and treachery do not always obtain that pitiful reward. The most useful ministers to the crown, and therefore the most likely to be employed, especially in great emergencies, are those who are best beloved by the people; and those only are beloved by the people, who act steadily and uniformly in support of their liberties. Patriots, therefore, have frequently, and especially upon important occasions, the best chance of being advanced to offices of profit and power. An abject compliance with the will of an imperious prince, and a ready disposition to sacrifice every duty to his pleasure, are sometimes, I confess, the steps, by which only men can expect to rise to wealth and titles. Let us suppose that, in this manner, they are successful in attaining them. Is the despicable prize a sufficient recompense, for submitting to the infamous means by which it was procured, and for the torturing remorse with which the possession of it must be accompanied? Will it compensate for the merited curses of the nation and of posterity?

These must be very strong checks upon the conduct of every man, who is not utterly lost to all sense of praise and blame. Few will expose themselves to the just abhorrence of those among whom they live, and to the excruciating sensations which such abhorrence must produce. . . .

What has been already advanced will suffice to show, that it is repugnant to the essential maxims of jurisprudence, to the ultimate end of all governments, to the genius of the British constitution, and to the liberty and happiness of the colonies, that they should be bound by the legislative authority of the parliament of Great Britain. 🙒

Notes*

a. 4. Bl. Com. 48. 49. [Sir William Blackstone, *Commentaries on the Laws of England*]

b. Id. 50. 51. [Ibid.]

c. The right of sovereignty is that of commanding finally—but in order to procure real felicity; for if this end is not obtained, sovereignty ceases to be a legitimate authority. 2. Burl. 32, 33. [Jean Jacques Burlamaqui, *The Principles of Natural and Political Law . . .*]

d. The law of nature is superiour in obligation to any other. 1. Bl. Com. 41. [Sir William Blackstone, *Commentaries on the Laws of England*]

e. 2. Burl. 19. [Jean Jacques Burlamaqui, *The Principles of Natural and Political Law . . .*]

f. Bol. Diss. on Part. I. 11. 12. p. 167. 179. [Henry St. John, Viscount Bolingbroke, *A Dissertation upon Parties . . .*]

g. As the law is the birthright of every subject, so wheresoever they go, they carry their laws with them. 2. P. Wms. 75. [William Peere Williams, *Reports of Cases, Court of Chancery . . .*]

h. 4. Ins. 25. [Sir Edward Coke, *The Institutes of the Laws of England*]

i. The commons of England have a great and considerable right in the government; and a share in the legislature without whom no law passes. 2. Ld. Ray. 950. [Sir Robert Raymond, First Baron, *Reports, King's Bench and Common Pleas*]

j. Sp. L. b. 2. c. 2. [Charles Louis de Secondat, Baron de la Brède et de Montesquieu, *The Spirit of Laws*]

k. The Athenians, justly jealous of this important privilege, punished, with death, every stranger who presumed to interfere in the assemblies of the people.

l. The English freedom will be at an end whenever the court invades the free election of parliament. Rapin. [Paul de Rapin-Thoyras, . . . *An Historical Dissertation upon Whig and Tory* . . .]

A right that a man has to give his vote at the election of a person to represent him in parliament, there to concur to the making of laws, which are to bind his liberty and property, is a most transcendant thing and of a high nature. 2. Ld. Ray. 953. [Sir Robert Raymond, First Baron, *Reports, King's Bench and Common Pleas*]

m. There are a few exceptions in the case of officers at will.

*The notes are Wilson's; his abbreviated titles have been expanded in brackets.

State House Yard Speech

From November 28 through December 11, 1787, Wilson dealt with the fury of the Anti-Federalists. They were determined to defeat the proposed ratification of the Constitution at the Pennsylvania ratifying convention. This would have been a crushing blow to the Constitution's chances. Wilson's arguments prevailed, and the vote was 61–23 in favor of ratification.

In the midst of the debates over ratification, on October 6, 1787, Wilson spoke in the State House yard to a large crowd of Pennsylvanians who were very concerned that the new federal government would abolish the states and exercise control over all Americans.

Wilson began his defense of the Constitution by discussing the origin of authority for the new government. He first described the powers given by the people to their state governments. He then compared the two grants of power—to the states and to the national government. He explained that in the case of the states "every thing which is not reserved is given" and in the case of the national government "every thing which is not given, is reserved." James Wilson's task was as difficult as it was simple—to allay the fears of the public. His answer, to put it simply: Why would the public need protection from a body that didn't have the power to infringe on their rights in the first place?

This speech may well have been crucial to the ratification of the Constitution by enough states to secure its adoption.

State Houſe Yard Speech

Mr. Chairman and Fellow Citizens, Having received the honor of an appointment to represent you in the late convention, it is perhaps, my duty to comply with the request of many gentlemen whose characters and judgments I sincerely respect, and who have urged, that this would be a proper occasion to lay before you any information which will serve to explain and elucidate the principles and arrangements of the constitution, that has been submitted to the consideration of the United States. I confess that I am unprepared for so extensive and so important a disquisition; but the insidious attempts which are clandestinely and industriously made to pervert and destroy the new plan, induce me the more readily to engage in its defence; and the impressions of four months constant attention to the subject, have not been so easily effaced as to leave me without an answer to the objections which have been raised.

It will be proper however, before I enter into the refutation of the charges that are alledged, to mark the leading descrimination between the state constitutions, and the constitution of the United States. When the people established the powers of legislation under their separate governments, they invested their representatives with every right and authority which they did not in explicit terms reserve; and therefore upon every question, respecting the jurisdiction of the house of assembly, if the frame of government is silent, the jurisdiction is efficient and complete. But in delegating foederal powers, another criterion was necessarily introduced, and the congressional authority is to be collected, not from tacit implication, but from the positive grant expressed in the instrument of union. Hence it is evident, that in the former case every thing which is not reserved is given, but in the latter the reverse of the proposition prevails, and every thing which is not given, is reserved. This distinction being recognized, will furnish an answer to those who think the omission of a bill of rights, a defect in the proposed constitution: for it would have been superfluous and absurd to have stipulated with a foederal body of our own creation, that we should enjoy those privileges, of which we are not divested either by the intention or the act, that has brought that body into existence. For instance, the liberty of the press, which has been a copious source of declamation and opposition, what controul can proceed from the foederal government to shackle or destroy that sacred palladium of national freedom? If indeed, a power similar to that which has been granted for the regulation of commerce, had been granted to regulate literary publications, it would have been as necessary to stipulate that the liberty of the press should be preserved inviolate, as that the impost should be general in its operation. With respect likewise to the particular district of ten miles, which is to be made the seat of foederal government, it will undoubtedly be proper to observe this salutary precaution, as there the legislative power will be exclusively lodged in the president, senate, and house of representatives of the United States. But this could not be an object with the convention, for it must naturally depend upon a future compact, to which the citizens immediately interested will, and ought to be parties; and there is no reason to suspect that so popular a privilege will in that case be neglected. In truth then, the proposed system possesses no influence whatever upon the press, and it would have been merely nugatory to have introduced a formal declaration upon the subject—nay, that very declaration might have been construed to imply that some degree of power was given, since we undertook to define its extent.

Another objection that has been fabricated against the new constitution, is expressed in this disingenuous form—"the trial by jury is abolished in civil cases." I must be excused, my fellow citizens, if upon this point, I take advantage of my professional experience to detect the futility of the assertion. Let it be remembered then, that the business of the Foederal Convention was not local, but general; not limited to the views and establishments of a single state, but co-extensive with the continent, and comprehending the views and establishments of thirteen independent sovereignties. When therefore, this subject was in discussion, we were involved in difficulties which pressed on all sides, and no precedent could be discovered to direct our course. The cases open to a trial by jury differed in the different states, it was therefore impracticable on that ground to have made a general rule. The want of uniformity would have rendered any reference to the practice of the states idle and useless; and it could not, with any propriety, be said that "the trial by jury shall be as heretofore," since there has never existed any foederal system of jurisprudence to which the declaration could relate.

Besides, it is not in all cases that the trial by jury is adopted in civil questions, for causes depending in courts of admiralty, such as relate to maritime captures, and such as are agitated in courts of equity, do not require the intervention of that tribunal. How then, was the line of discrimination to be drawn? The convention found the task too difficult for them, and they left the business as it stands, in the fullest confidence that no danger could possibly ensue, since the proceedings of the supreme court, are to be regulated by the congress, which is a faithful representation of the people; and the oppression of government is effectually barred, by declaring that in all criminal cases the trial by jury shall be preserved.

This constitution, it has been further urged, is of a pernicious tendency, because it tolerates a standing army in the time of peace.—This has always been a topic of popular declamation; and yet, I do not know a nation in the world, which has not found it necessary and useful to maintain the appearance of strength in a season of the most profound tranquility. Nor is it a novelty with us; for under the present articles of confederation, congress certainly possesses this reprobated power, and the exercise of that power is proved at this moment by her cantonments along the banks of the Ohio. But what would be our national situation were it otherwise? Every principle of policy must be subverted, and the government must declare war, before they are prepared to carry it on. Whatever may be the provocation, however important the object in view, and however necessary dispatch and secrecy may be, still the declaration must precede the preparation, and the enemy will be informed of your intention, not only before you are equipped for an attack, but even before you are fortified for a defence. The consequence is too obvious to require any further delineation, and no man, who regards the dignity and safety of his country, can deny the necessity of a military force, under the controul and with the restrictions which the new constitution provides.

Perhaps there never was a charge made with less reasons than that which predicts the institution of a baneful aristocracy in the foederal senate. This body branches into two characters, the one legislative, and the other executive. In its legislative character it can effect no purpose, without the cooperation of the house of representatives, and in its executive character, it can accomplish no object, without the concurrence of the president. Thus fettered, I do not know any act which the senate can of itself perform, and such dependance necessarily precludes every idea of influence and superiority. But I will confess that in the organization of this body, a compromise between contending interests is descernible; and when we reflect how various are the laws, commerce, habits, population, and extent of the confederated states, this evidence of mutual concession and accommodation ought rather to command a generous applause, than to excite jealousy and reproach. For my part, my admiration can only be equalled by my astonishment, in beholding so perfect a system, formed from such heterogeneous materials.

The next accusation I shall consider, is that which represents the foederal constitution as not only calculated, but designedly framed, to reduce the state governments to mere corporations, and eventually to annihilate them. Those who have employed the term corporation upon this occasion, are not perhaps aware of its extent. In common parlance, indeed, it is generally applied to petty associations for the ease and conveniency of a few individuals; but in its enlarged sense, it will comprehend the government of Pennsylvania, the existing union of the states, and even this projected system is nothing more than a formal act of incorporation. But upon what pretence can it be alledged that it was designed to annihilate the state governments? For, I will undertake to prove that upon their existence, depends the existence of the foederal plan. For this purpose, permit me to call your attention to the manner in which the president, senate, and house of representatives, are proposed to be appointed. The president is to be chosen by electors, nominated in such manner as the legislature of each state may direct; so that if there is no legislature, there can be no electors, and consequently the office of president cannot be supplied. The senate is to be composed of two senators from each state, chosen by the legislature; and therefore if there is no legislature, there can be no senate. The house of representatives, is to be composed of members chosen every second year by the people of the several states, and the electors in each state shall have the qualifications requisite for electors of the most numerous branch of the state legislature,—unless therefore, there is a state legislature, that qualification cannot be ascertained, and the popular branch of the foederal constitution must likewise be extinct. From this view, then it is evidently absurd to suppose, that the annihilation of the separate governments will result from their union; or, that having that intention, the authors of the new system would have bound their connection with such indissoluble ties. Let me here advert to an arrangement highly advantageous, for you will perceive, without prejudice to the powers of the legislature in the election of senators, the people at large will acquire an additional privilege in returning members to the house of representatives—whereas, by the present confederation, it is the legislature alone that appoints the delegates to Congress.

The power of direct taxation has likewise been treated as an improper delegation to the foederal government; but when we consider it as the duty of that body to provide for the national safety, to support the dignity of the union, and to discharge the debts contracted upon the collective faith of the states for their common benefit, it must be acknowledged, that those upon whom such important obligations are imposed, ought in justice and in policy to possess every means requisite for a faithful performance of their trust. But why should we be alarmed with visionary evils? I will venture to predict, that the great revenue of the United States must, and always will be raised by impost, for, being at once less obnoxious, and more productive, the interest of the government will be best promoted by the accommodation of the people. Still however, the objects of direct taxation should be within reach in all cases of emergency; and there is no more reason to apprehend oppression in the mode of collecting a revenue from this resource, than in the form of an impost, which, by universal assent, is left to the authority of the foederal government. In either case, the force of civil institutions will be adequate to the purpose; and the dread of military violence, which has been assiduously disseminated, must eventually prove the mere effusion of a wild imagination, or a factious spirit. But the salutary consequences that must flow from thus enabling the government to receive and support the credit of the union, will afford another answer to the objections upon this ground. The State of Pennsylvania particularly, which has encumbered itself with the assumption of a great proportion of the public debt, will derive considerable relief and advantage; for, as it was the imbecility of the present confederation, which gave rise to the funding law, that law must naturally expire, when a competent and energetic foederal system shall be substituted—the state will then be discharged from an extraordinary burthen, and the national creditor will find it to be his interest to return to his original security.

After all, my fellow citizens, it is neither extraordinary or unexpected, that the constitution offered to your consideration, should meet with opposition. It is the nature of man to pursue his own interest, in preference to the public good; and I do not mean to make any personal reflection, when I add, that it is the interest of a very numerous, powerful, and respectable body to counteract and destroy the excellent work produced by the late convention. All the offices of government, and all the appointments for the administration of justice and the collection of the public revenue, which are transferred from the individual to the aggregate sovereignty of the states, will necessarily turn the stream of influence and emolument into a new channel. Every person therefore, who either enjoys, or expects to enjoy, a place of profit under the present establishment, will object to the proposed innovation; not, in truth, because it is injurious to the liberties of his country, but because it affects his schemes of wealth and consequence. I will confess indeed, that I am not a blind admirer of this plan of government, and that there are some parts of it, which if my wish had prevailed, would certainly have been altered. But, when I reflect how widely men differ in their opinions, and that every man (and the observation applies likewise to every state) has an equal pretension to assert his own, I am satisfied that any thing nearer to perfection could not have been accomplished. If there are errors, it should be remembered, that the seeds of reformation are sown in the work itself, and the concurrence of two thirds of the congress may at any time introduce alterations and amendments. Regarding it then, in every point of view, with a candid and disinterested mind, I am bold to assert, that it is the best form of government which has ever been offered to the world. 🌿

Oration Delivered on the Fourth of July 1788

Wilson's final act in the process of framing and inaugurating the U.S. Constitution came on July 4, 1788, when a great procession took place in Philadelphia. Ten gentlemen, walking arm in arm, represented the ten states that had so far ratified the Constitution. To Wilson fell the honor of representing Pennsylvania.

The central feature of the celebration was an oration delivered by Wilson. Packed with erudite classical allusions, it did not reveal any new dimension to his political thought, but it repeated, in a more general and popular form, arguments he had already used. Wilson emphasized what he had always said was crucial to the success of the new system—the duty of the citizens to participate responsibly in the process of government.

ORATION DELIVERED

on the Fourth of July 1788, at the Proceſſion
Formed at Philadelphia to Celebrate the
Adoption of the Conſtitution
OF THE UNITED STATES

My friends and fellow citizens,

Your candid and generous indulgence I may well bespeak, for many reasons. I shall mention but one. While I express it, I feel it in all its force. My abilities are unequal—abilities far superiour to mine would be unequal—to the occasion on which I have the honour of being called to address you.

A people free and enlightened, establishing and ratifying a system of government, which they have previously considered, examined, and approved! This is the spectacle, which we are assembled to celebrate; and it is the most dignified one that has yet appeared on our globe. Numerous and splendid have been the triumphs of conquerors. But from what causes have they originated?—Of what consequences have they been productive? They have generally begun in ambition: they have generally ended in tyranny. But nothing tyrannical can participate of dignity: and to freedom's eye, Sesostris himself appears contemptible, even when he treads on the necks of kings.

The senators of Rome, seated on their curule chairs, and surrounded with all their official lustre, were an object much more respectable: and we view, without displeasure, the admiration of those untutored savages, who considered them as so many gods upon earth. But who were those senators? They were only a part of a society: they were vested only with inferiour powers.

What is the object exhibited to our contemplation? A whole people exercising its first and greatest power—performing an act of sovereignty, original and unlimited!

The scene before us is unexampled as well as magnificent. The greatest part of governments have been the deformed offspring of force and fear.

With these we deign not comparison. But there have been others which have formed bold pretensions to higher regard. You have heard of Sparta, of Athens, and of Rome; you have heard of their admired constitutions, and of their high-prized freedom. In fancied right of these, they conceived themselves to be elevated above the rest of the human race, whom they marked with the degrading title of barbarians. But did they, in all their pomp and pride of liberty, ever furnish, to the astonished world, an exhibition similar to that which we now contemplate? Were their constitutions framed by those, who were appointed for that purpose, by the people? After they were framed, were they submitted to the consideration of the people? Had the people an opportunity of expressing their sentiments concerning them? Were they to stand or fall by the people's approving or rejecting vote? To all these questions, attentive and impartial history obliges us to answer in the negative. The people were either unfit to be trusted, or their lawgivers were too ambitious to trust them.

The far-famed establishment of Lycurgus was introduced by deception and fraud. Under the specious pretence of consulting the oracle concerning his laws, he prevailed on the Spartans to make a temporary experiment of them during his absence, and to swear that they would suffer no alteration of them till his return. Taking a disingenuous advantage of their scrupulous regard for their oaths, he prevented his return by a voluntary death, and, in this manner, endeavoured to secure a proud immortality to his system.

Even Solon—the mild and moderating Solon—far from considering himself as employed only to *propose* such regulations as he should think best calculated for promoting the happiness of the commonwealth, made and promulgated his laws with all the haughty airs of absolute power. On more occasions than one, we find him boasting, with much selfcomplacency, of his extreme forbearance and condescension, because he did not establish a despotism in his own favour, and because he did not reduce his equals to the humiliating condition of his slaves.

Did Numa submit his institutions to the good sense and free investigation of Rome? They were received in precious communications from the goddess Egeria, with whose presence and regard he was supremely favoured; and they were imposed on the easy faith of the citizens, as the dictates of an inspiration that was divine.

Such, my fellow citizens, was the origin of the most splendid establishments that have been hitherto known; and such were the arts, to which they owed their introduction and success.

What a flattering contrast arises from a retrospect of the scenes which we now commemorate! Delegates were appointed to deliberate and propose. They met and performed their delegated trust. The result of their deliberations was laid before the people. It was discussed and scrutinized in the fullest, freest, and severest manner—by speaking, by writing, and by printing—by individuals and by publick bodies—by its friends and by its enemies. What was the issue? Most favourable and most glorious to the system. In state after state, at time after time, it was ratified—in some states unanimously—on the whole, by a large and very respectable majority.

It would be improper now to examine its qualities. A decent respect for those who have accepted it, will lead us to presume that it is worthy of their acceptance. The deliberate ratifications, which have taken place, at once recommend the system, and the people by whom it has been ratified.

But why, methinks I hear some one say—why is so much exultation displayed in celebrating this event? We are prepared to give the reasons of our joy. We rejoice, because, under this constitution, we hope to see just government, and to enjoy the blessings that walk in its train.

Let us begin with Peace—the mild and modest harbinger of felicity! How seldom does the amiable wanderer choose, for her permanent residence, the habitations of men! In their systems, she sees too many arrangements, civil and ecclesiastical, inconsistent with the calmness and benignity of her temper. In the old world, how many millions of men do we behold, unprofitable to society, burthensome to industry, the props of establishments that deserve not to be supported, the causes of distrust in the times of peace, and the instruments of destruction in the times of war? Why are they not employed in cultivating useful arts, and in forwarding publick improvements? Let us indulge the pleasing expectation, that such will be the operation of government in the United States. Why may we not hope, that, disentangled from the intrigues and jealousies of European politicks, and unmolested with the alarm and solicitude to which these intrigues and jealousies give birth, our counsels will be directed to the encouragement, and our strength will be exerted in the cultivation, of all the arts of peace?

Of these, the first is agriculture. This is true in all countries: in the United States, its truth is of peculiar importance. The subsistence of man, the materials of manufactures, the articles of commerce—all spring originally from the soil. On agriculture, therefore, the wealth of nations is founded. Whether we consult the observations that reason will suggest, or attend to the information that history will give, we shall, in each case, be satisfied of the influence of government, good or bad, upon the state of agriculture. In a government, whose maxims are those of oppression, property is insecure. It is given, it is taken away, by caprice. Where there is no security for property, there is no encouragement for industry. Without industry, the richer the soil, the more it abounds with weeds. The evidence of history warrants the truth of these general remarks. Attend to Greece; and compare her agriculture in ancient and in modern times. Then, smiling harvests bore testimony to the bountiful boons of liberty. Now, the very earth languishes under oppression. View the Campania of Rome. How melancholy the prospect! Whichever way you turn your afflicted eyes, scenes of desolation crowd before them. Waste and barrenness appear around you in all their hideous forms. What is the reason? With double tyranny the land is cursed. Open the classick page: you trace, in chaste description, the beautiful reverse of every thing you have seen. Whence proceeds the difference? When that description was made, the force of liberty pervaded the soil.

But is agriculture the only art, which feels the influence of government? Over manufactures and commerce its power is equally prevalent. There the same causes operate—and there they produce the same effects. The industrious village, the busy city, the crowded port—all these are the gifts of liberty; and without a good government, liberty cannot exist.

These are advantages, but these are not all the advantages, that result from a system of good government.—Agriculture, manufactures, and commerce will ensure to us plenty, convenience, and elegance. But is there not something still wanting to finish the man? Are internal virtues and accomplishments less estimable, or less attracting than external arts and ornaments? Is the operation of government less powerful upon the former than upon the latter? By no means. Upon this as upon a preceding topick, reason and history will concur in their information and advice. In a serene mind, the sciences and the virtues love to dwell. But can the mind of a man be serene, when the property, liberty, subsistence of himself, and of those for whom he feels more than he feels for himself, depend on a tyrant's nod. If the dispirited subject of oppression can, with difficulty, exert his enfeebled faculties, so far as to provide, on the incessant demands of nature, food just enough to lengthen out his wretched existence, can it be expected that, in such a state, he will experience those fine and vigorous movements of the soul, without the full and free exercise of which, science and virtue will never flourish? Look around you to the nations that now exist. View, in historick retrospect, the nations that have heretofore existed. The collected result will be, an entire conviction of these all-interesting truths—where tyranny reigns, there is the country of ignorance and vice—where good government prevails, there is the country of science and virtue. Under a good government, therefore, we must look for the accomplished man.

But shall we confine our views even here? While we wish to be accomplished men and citizens, shall we wish to be nothing more? While we perform our duty, and promote our happiness in this world, shall we bestow no regards upon the next? Does no connexion subsist between the two? From this connexion flows the most important of all the blessings of good government. But here let us pause—unassisted reason can guide us no farther—she directs us to that heaven-descended science, by which life and immortality have been brought to light.

May we not now say, that we have reason for our joy? But while we cherish the delightful emotion, let us remember those things, which are requisite to give it permanence and stability. Shall we lie supine, and look in listless langour, for those blessings and enjoyments, to which exertion is inseparably attached? If we would be happy, we must be active. The constitution and our manners must mutually support and be supported. Even on this festivity, it will not be disagreeable or incongruous to review the virtues and manners that both justify and adorn it.

Frugality and temperance first attract our attention. These simple but powerful virtues are the sole foundation, on which a good government can rest with security. They were the virtues, which nursed and educated infant Rome, and prepared her for all her greatness. But in the giddy hour of her prosperity, she spurned from her the obscure instruments, by which it was procured; and, in their place, substituted luxury and dissipation. The consequence was such as might have been expected. She preserved, for some time, a gay and flourishing appearance; but the internal health and soundness of her constitution were gone. At last, she fell a victim to the poisonous draughts, which were administered by her perfidious favourites. The fate of Rome, both in her rising and in her falling state, will be the fate of every other nation that shall follow both parts of her example.

Industry appears next among the virtues of a good citizen. Idleness is the nurse of villains. The industrious alone constitute a nation's strength. I will not expatiate on this fruitful subject. Let one animating reflection suffice. In a well constituted commonwealth, the industry of every citizen extends beyond himself. A common interest pervades the society. Each gains from all, and all gain from each. It has often been observed, that the sciences flourish all together: the remark applies equally to the arts.

Your patriotick feelings attest the truth of what I say, when, among the virtues necessary to merit and preserve the advantages of a good government, I number a warm and uniform attachment to liberty, and to the constitution. The enemies of liberty are artful and insidious. A counterfeit steals her dress, imitates her manner, forges her signature, assumes her name. But the real name of the deceiver is licentiousness. Such is her effrontery, that she will charge liberty to her face with imposture: and she will, with shameless front, insist that herself alone is the genuine character, and that herself alone is entitled to the respect, which the genuine character deserves. With the giddy and undiscerning, on whom a deeper impression is made by dauntless impudence than by modest merit, her pretensions are often successful. She receives the honours of liberty, and liberty herself is treated as a traitor and a usurper. Generally, however, this bold impostor acts only a secondary part. Though she alone appear upon the stage, her motions are regulated by dark ambition, who sits concealed behind the curtain, and who knows that despotism, his other favourite, can always follow the success of licentiousness. Against these enemies of liberty, who act in concert, though they appear on opposite sides, the patriot citizen will keep a watchful guard.

A good constitution is the greatest blessing, which a society can enjoy. Need I infer, that it is the duty of every citizen to use his best and most unremitting endeavours for preserving it pure, healthful, and vigorous?

For the accomplishment of this great purpose, the exertions of no one citizen are unimportant. Let no one, therefore, harbour, for a moment, the mean idea, that he is and can be of no value to his country: let the contrary manly impression animate his soul. Every one can, at *many* times, perform, to the state, *useful* services; and he, who steadily pursues the road of patriotism, has the most inviting prospect of being able, at *some* times, to perform *eminent* ones. Allow me to direct your attention, in a very particular manner, to a momentous part, which, by this constitution, every citizen will frequently be called to act. All those in places of power and trust will be elected either immediately by the people, or in such a manner that their appointment will depend ultimately on such immediate election. All the derivative movements of government must spring from the original movement of the people at large. If to this they give a sufficient force and a just direction, all the others will be governed by its controlling power. To speak without a metaphor, if the people, at their elections, take care to choose none but representatives that are wise and good, their representatives will take care, in their turn, to choose or appoint none but such as are wise and good also. The remark applies to every succeeding election and appointment. Thus the characters proper for publick officers will be diffused from the immediate elections of the people over the remotest parts of administration. Of what immense consequence is it, then, that this primary duty should be faithfully and skilfully discharged! On the faithful and skilful discharge of it, the publick happiness or infelicity, under this and every other constitution, must, in a very great measure, depend. For, believe me, no government, even the best, can be happily administered by ignorant or vicious men. You will forgive me, I am sure, for endeavouring to impress upon your minds, in the strongest manner, the importance of this great duty. It is the first concoction in politicks; and if an errour is committed here, it can never be corrected in any subsequent process: the certain consequence must be disease. Let no one say, that he is but a single citizen; and that his ticket will be but one in the box. That one ticket may turn the election. In battle, every soldier should consider the publick safety as depending on his single arm: at an election, every citizen should consider the publick happiness as depending on his single vote.

A progressive state is necessary to the happiness and perfection of man. Whatever attainments are already reached, attainments still higher should be pursued. Let us, therefore, strive with noble emulation. Let us suppose we have done nothing, while any thing yet remains to be done. Let us, with fervent zeal, press forward, and make unceasing advances in every thing that can support, improve, refine, or embellish society. To enter into particulars under each of these heads, and to dilate them according to their importance, would be improper at this time. A few remarks on the last of them will be congenial with the entertainments of this auspicious day.

If we give the slightest attention to nature, we shall discover, that with utility, she is curious to blend ornament. Can we imitate a better pattern? Publick exhibitions have been the favourite amusements of some of the wisest and most accomplished nations. Greece, in her most shining era, considered her games as far from being the least respectable among her publick establishments. The shows of the circus evince that, on this subject, the sentiments of Greece were fortified by those of Rome.

Publick processions may be so planned and executed as to join both the properties of nature's rule. They may instruct and improve, while they entertain and please. They may point out the elegance or usefulness of the sciences and the arts. They may preserve the memory, and engrave the importance of great political events. They may represent, with peculiar felicity and force, the operation and effects of great political truths. The picturesque and splendid decorations around me furnish the most beautiful and most brilliant proofs, that these remarks are far from being imaginary.

The commencement of our government has been eminently glorious: let our progress in every excellence be proportionably great. It will—it must be so. What an enrapturing prospect opens on the United States! Placid husbandry walks in front, attended by the venerable plough. Lowing herds adorn our vallies: bleating flocks spread over our hills: verdant meadows, enamelled pastures, yellow harvests, bending orchards, rise in rapid succession from east to west. Plenty, with her copious horn, sits easy smiling, and, in conscious complacency, enjoys and presides over the scenes. Commerce next advances in all her splendid and embellished forms. The rivers, and lakes, and seas, are crowded with ships. Their shores are covered with cities. The cities are filled with inhabitants. The arts, decked with elegance, yet with simplicity, appear in beautiful variety, and well adjusted arrangement. Around them are diffused, in rich abundance, the necessaries, the decencies, and the ornaments of life. With heartfelt contentment, industry beholds his honest labours flourishing and secure. Peace walks serene and unalarmed over all the unmolested regions—while liberty, virtue, and religion go hand in hand, harmoniously, protecting, enlivening, and exalting all! Happy country! May thy happiness be perpetual! 🙵

Suggested Readings

Beeman, Richard. *Plain, Honest Men: The Making of the American Constitution.* New York: Random House, 2009.

Hall, Mark David. *The Political and Legal Philosophy of James Wilson, 1742–1798.* Columbia, MO: University of Missouri Press, 1997.

Larson, Edward J., and Michael P. Winship. *The Constitutional Convention: A Narrative History from the Notes of James Madison.* New York: Modern Library, 2005.

Maier, Pauline. *Ratification: The People Debate the Constitution, 1787–1788.* New York: Simon & Schuster, 2010.

Pascal, Jean-Marc. *The Political Ideas of James Wilson: 1742–1798.* New York: Garland, 1991.

Rakove, Jack N. *Original Meanings: Politics and Ideas in the Making of the Constitution.* New York: Alfred A. Knopf, 1997.

Smith, Charles Page. *James Wilson: Founding Father, 1742–1798.* Chapel Hill, NC: University of North Carolina Press, 1956.

Wood, Gordon S. *The Idea of America: Reflections on the Birth of the United States.* New York: Penguin, 2011.

About Maynard Garrison

Maynard Garrison's graduation from Princeton University, New Jersey, in 1950 was followed by law school and forty years of practicing law in San Francisco, California. His dedication to St. Andrews, Scotland, and James Wilson began with the chance reading of Andrew Bennett's pamphlet *James Wilson of St. Andrews: An American Statesman, 1742–1798*. Garrison collected the *Collected Works of James Wilson*, published in two volumes by the Liberty Fund in 2007. He is the American advisor to the James Wilson Doctoral Programme in Constitutional Studies at the University of St. Andrews.

About the Colonial Williamsburg Foundation

The Colonial Williamsburg Foundation is a private, not-for-profit educational institution that preserves and interprets the eighteenth-century capital of Virginia. In addition to the Historic Area, the Foundation operates the DeWitt Wallace Decorative Arts Museum, the Abby Aldrich Rockefeller Folk Art Museum, Bassett Hall, and the John D. Rockefeller, Jr. Library.

Colonial Williamsburg actively supports history and citizenship education through a wide variety of educational outreach programs. Programs for students include *The Idea of America*, an interactive, fully digital, Web-based curriculum for high school students, and Electronic Field Trips, which transport students from across the country into American history. Programs for teachers include the Williamsburg Teacher Institute and workshops in school districts across the country.